SPEAK
TO THE WINDS

SPEAK proverbs from africa
TO THE WINDS

Kofi Asare Opoku

illustrated by Dindga McCannon

Lothrop, Lee & Shepard Company | New York

Grateful acknowledgment is made to the following authors and publishers for permission to use material from their books:

Chinua Achebe, *No Longer at Ease* (London, William Heinemann, Ltd., 1963) and *Arrow of God* (London, William Heinemann, Ltd., 1964).

C. A. Akrofi, *Twi Proverbs,* (London and Basingstoke, Macmillan, 1948).

G. Barra, *1000 Kikuyu Proverbs* (London and Basingstoke, Macmillan, 1960).

Isaac O. Delano, *Owe L'Esin Oro* (London, Oxford University Press, 1966).

E. B. Idowu, *Olodumare: God in Yoruba Belief* (London, Longman's Group Ltd. and New York, Frederick A. Praeger and Co., Inc., 1962).

Laurens van der Post, William Morrow & Co., Inc., and The Hogarth Press, Ltd. for five proverbs reprinted by permission of William Morrow & Co., Inc. and the Hogarth Press, Ltd. from *A Story Like the Wind,* copyright © 1972 by Laurens van der Post.

Copyright © 1975 by Kofi Asare Opoku

Library of Congress Cataloging in Publication Data

Opoku, Kofi Asare, comp.
  Speak to the winds.

  SUMMARY: A collection of African proverbs primarily from Ghana, dealing with wisdom, truth and falsehood, human conduct, contentment, opportunity, children, and animals.
  1. Proverbs, African—Juvenile literature.
[1. Proverbs, African] I. McCannon, Dindga, ill. II. Title.
PN6519.A6066   398.9'667   74-22468
ISBN 0-688-41688-8
ISBN 0-688-51688-2 lib. bdg.

To my parents, whose lives opened
my eyes to the wisdom of our forefathers.

contents

introduction

African proverbs express the wisdom of the African people and are a key to the understanding of African ways of life in the past and in the present.

All people are believed to possess wisdom and the Akan people of Ghana tell an interesting story of how it spread to all parts of the world:

Long, long ago there lived a man called Kwaku Ananse, who had a wife, Nkonore Yaa, and a son, Ntikuma. Ananse possessed all the wisdom in the world, but so selfish was he that he did not want to share it with anybody. He decided to collect it into a big pot and hide it at the top of a big, tall tree in the forest. Ananse's wife got him the largest pot she could find, and Ananse began to fill it up. He told no one what he was doing.

When he had finished, he fastened a rope around the pot, tied the rest of it around his neck, and sneaked out of the house in the dead of night,

the pot hanging on his belly. Ananse walked
clumsily into the thickest part of the forest until
he came to the tree which he thought would serve
his purpose, and stopped.

Ananse did not think that any of the members
of his house had seen him, but he was mistaken. His
son had been awakened by the noise his father
made and had followed Ananse, curious to see
just what Ananse was going to do. He hid himself
behind a tree, a good distance away, and gazed
intently at his father.

After pausing for awhile to steady the pot,
Ananse began to climb the tree. But with the pot in
front of him it was very difficult for him to get
a good grip on the trunk. He tried several times to
climb the tree but could not and so he paused to
think.

As Ananse scratched his head in search of a
solution to his problem, he was startled by a loud

laugh behind him and he turned around to find, to his utter amazement, his son. Ntikuma suggested to his father that if he would put the pot on his back instead of on his belly he would find it easier to climb the tree.

Ananse was furious that it took his son to show him this simple solution. Filled with great frustration, he threw down the pot and the wisdom from it spread to all parts of the world.

It is part of this wisdom, scattered from Ananse's pot which appears in the African proverbs found in this book.

Proverbs have many uses in African societies: they may express an eternal truth; they may be a warning against foolish acts or be a guide to good conduct. They may also bring special meaning to certain situations and may even solve particular problems.

Proverbs are not only expressed in words,

but also in the language of the drums and the sound
of the horns blown by the attendants of our chiefs.
Even patterns woven in cloth by our weavers
may express proverbial sayings, such as the
Kente pattern, *"Ti koro nko agyina,"*—"One head
does not go into council," (it is better if two
heads make a decision) which the Republic of
Ghana presented to the United Nations, and may
be seen hanging on one of the walls in the
delegates' lounge in the United Nations Building
in New York.

The Yoruba of Nigeria emphasize the value of
proverbs by saying that, "A proverb is the horse
which can carry one swiftly to the discovery
of ideas." It is hoped that this small collection will
give readers a little insight into an important
aspect of our African cultural heritage and help
to increase human understanding.

11

CHILDREN

A child breaks a snail shell, but does not break
a tortoise shell

children

1. There is no wealth where there are no children.

2. We work because of our children.

3. A child breaks a snail shell, but does not break a tortoise shell.

4. A child does not laugh at the hunchback.

5. When a child does what a grown-up person does, the child sees what a grown-up sees.

6. When children learn to wash their hands, they may eat with their elders.

7. A child may have as many clothes as its father, but it does not have as many rags.

8. An elder does not roast a hot stone and place it in the hands of the child.

9. Children are the gift of God.

10. A child is:
    The one who gives us honor
    The one who covers us more than
        clothing
    The one who gives us the boldness to
        speak in a gathering.

11. Nothing is as painful as when one dies without leaving a child behind.

WISDOM

A fool's walking stick helps the wise person
to stand

wisdom

1. Wisdom is not like money which should be kept in a safe.

2. Wisdom outweighs strength.

3. If you are greedy in conversation, you lose the wisdom of your friend.

4. You send a wise person on an important mission, not a long-legged person.

5. The wise person who does not learn ceases to be wise.

6. All knowledge is acquired by learning.

18

7. It is through other people's wisdom that we learn wisdom ourselves; a single person's understanding does not amount to anything.

8. If you say you know everything, you will sleep in a fool's hallway.

9. One must come out of one's house to begin learning.

10. A fool's walking stick helps the wise person to stand.

TRUTH AND FALSEHOOD

Whereas a liar takes a thousand years to go
on a journey, the one who speaks the truth
follows and overtakes the liar in a day

truth and falsehood

1. There is no fraud in truth.

2. Truth came to the market and could not be sold; we buy lies with ready cash.

3. If you sow falsehood, you reap deceit.

22

4. Whereas a liar takes a thousand years to go on a journey, the one who speaks the truth follows and overtakes the liar in a day.

5. If you travel with fraud, you may reach your destination but will be unable to return.

23

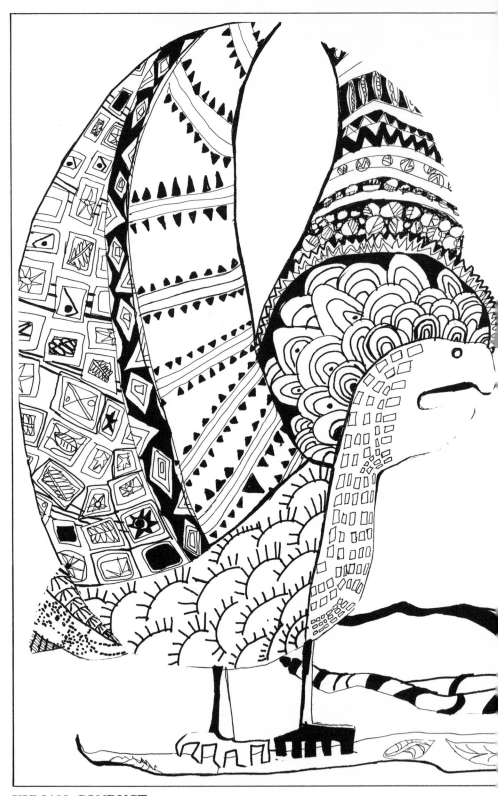

HUMAN CONDUCT

Even the greatest bird must come down from
the sky to find a tree to roost upon

human conduct

1. If the chief does not fight, the slave runs away.

2. If you do not forgive a crime, you commit a crime.

3. If you see wrong-doing or evil and say nothing against it, you become its victim.

4. One wicked person in a state hurts others.

5. The saying is, "Visit a foreign country and respect its citizens," and not "Visit a foreign country and act better than its citizens."

6. If you trample on another person's property in looking for your own, you will never find your own.

7. If you poison another, some of the poison gets into your own mouth.

8. If you build a poor wooden bridge across the river, it never rots until you have to cross it yourself.

9. There are no gods to support a lazy person; one's greatest support is one's own arm.

10. One who refuses to obey cannot command.

11. Wickedness begets remorse.

12. Those who are the cause of their own troubles never come to the end of them; but those who are troubled by other people do.

13. When a fowl is eating your neighbor's corn, drive it away or some day it will eat yours.

14. It is easier to put out the fire in the house of neighbors than to deal with the smoke in one's own.

15. Even the greatest bird must come down from the sky to find a tree to roost upon.

16. It is one's deeds that are counted, not one's years.

VIRTUE

The calabash of the kind breaks not, the
dish of the kind splits not. Both money and
children flow into the house of the kind

virtue

1. When virtue founds a town, the town grows and lasts long.

2. Goodness is hidden, but eventually appears.

3. The seed of goodness is as difficult to sow as it is hard to uproot the plant.

4. To possess virtue is better than to own gold.

5. Goodness and honesty share a common clan: they are like the halves of a growing kola nut which share an inseparable link.

6. Kindliness is like a loan, it is not a gift.

7. The calabash of the kind breaks not, the dish of the kind splits not. Both money and children flow into the house of the kind.

COOPERATION

The hand of the child cannot reach the shelf,
nor can the hand of the adult get through
the neck of a gourd

cooperation

1. A single hand cannot lift the calabash to the head.

2. A single peg cannot stretch out a skin.

3. When the right hand washes the left and the left hand washes the right, then both hands will be clean.

4. The hand of the child cannot reach the shelf, nor can the hand of the adult get through the neck of a gourd.

5. If your parents take care of you until you finish teething, you must also take care of them when they lose their teeth.

6. One strong person cannot close the ford of a river alone.

CONTENTMENT

Good fellowship is sharing good things
with friends

contentment

1. One does not carry elephant meat on the head and try to turn a cricket's hole with the foot.

2. To own only a few things is better than to be a thief.

3. If a quantity of water does not suffice for a bath, it will at least be sufficient for drinking.

4. Good fellowship is sharing good things with friends.

5. If poor people have nothing else, they at least
    have a tongue with which to defer payment
    of their debts.

6. To till the land is to love oneself.

7. The person who has not a small bag has at least
    a small basket.

8. The string can be useful until a rope can
    be found.

39

OPPORTUNITY

One should not ignore an elephant and throw
stones at a small bird

opportunity

1. One should not ignore an elephant and throw stones at a small bird.

2. One should not see fortune and seize it and let it go and then say, "If I had known."

3. One does not make a shield in the battlefield.

4. The one who asks the way does not get lost.

5. To move slowly is sometimes more advantageous than to go speedily.

6. Those who live near the Niger should not wash their hands in spittle.

7. One does not argue at the side of the stream whether a soap lathers or not.

8. One does not throw the stick after the snake has gone.

9. One does not begin to herd the cattle after it has been killed by lions.

HUMAN BEINGS

One who has family and friends is richer
than one who has money

human beings

1. It is the human being who counts: call on gold, gold does not respond; call on clothes, clothes do not respond; it is the human being who counts.

2. Even though the sound of the horn is unpleasant, it is being produced by a human being.

3. A house containing a bad person is better than an empty one.

4. Lack of companionship is worse than poverty.

5. May death not kill the person who tortures us, may the gods protect the one who ill-treats us; however long it takes our destiny to give us victory.

6. One who has family and friends is richer than one who has money.

7. People are the home.

8. One who has many friends is not caught by darkness in the road.

NATURE

If you want to speak to God,
speak to the winds

nature

1. If you want to speak to God, speak to the winds.

2. The rain forms dark clouds in the sky for the sake of those who are deaf, it rumbles for the sake of the blind.

3. It is God who drives away the flies for the tailless animal.

4. If God did not give the swallow any other gift, He gave her the gift of swiftness of movement.

5. Because the crab lives near the river it knows the language of the river.

6. When two antelopes are fighting and a lion approaches, the antelopes run off together (forgetting their quarrel).

7. When a dog says it will catch an elephant for you, it is deceiving you.

8. If the mouse were the size of a cow, it would be the cat's slave nevertheless.

9. If plain water were satisfying enough, then fish would not take the hook.

10. The goat says, "What will come has already come". (There is nothing new under the sun).

11. However poor the crocodile becomes, it hunts in the river, not in the forest.

12. Even the white ants confer before they scatter.

13. The tortoise is breathing, but its shell prevents people from seeing it.

14. It is through sheer stupidity and inexperience that a rat challenges a cat to a fight.

GENERAL PROVERBS

The warrior fights with courage,
not with excessive anger

general proverbs

1. To get the warmth of the fire one must stir the embers.

2. To forget is the same as to throw away.

3. To be hard does not mean to be hard as stone, and to be soft does not mean to be soft as water.

4. People count what they are refused, not what they are given.

5. One who warms oneself at the fire while the sun is shining does so for some reason.

6. The ears of the chief are like a strainer; there are more than a thousand openings to them.

7. The warrior fights with courage, not with excessive anger.

8. When deeds speak, words are nothing.

9. One who fetches water at the same place on the riverbank too often ends up in the crocodile.

10. Love exceeds reward.

11. Life is riches.

PROVERBS FROM REGALIA

proverbs from regalia: especially linguist staffs

At the court of Ghanaian chiefs, there is an important official, called "Okyeame", a linguist or spokesman, through whom the chief speaks to his elders and people, and is in turn spoken to, on both private and public occasions. The practice of speaking through a linguist after considered thought keeps a chief from speaking hastily or angrily in public.

The linguist is a wise man and is a close adviser to the chief. He advises on traditional law and custom, pronounces judgment at the court of law on behalf of the chief and generally deals with all matters of protocol. On account of his wisdom and eloquence, the linguist also serves as an ambassador to the chief.

Each linguist has a staff of office which is carved

in wood and topped with a symbolic emblem,
which is also covered with silver or gold leaf.
The emblem depicts a proverb or expresses a highly
cherished value in the society; it may also
represent a historic incident in the life of the state,
or even symbolize the qualities of the chief.

Below are some linguist staff tops and the values
they express:

1. POWER AND HOW TO HANDLE IT:
    A hand holding an egg—"Power must be
    handled in the manner of holding an egg in the
    hand: if you hold it too firmly it breaks;
    if you hold it too loosely it drops."

2. COOPERATION:
   A man attempting to scrape bark medicine
   from a tree—"When one person attempts to
   scrape bark medicine from a tree by himself, he
   always finds that the shavings fall out of his
   receptacle."

3. CONTENTMENT:
   A snail—"It is the snail that says, 'Let me be
   where I am; I am content with it.'"

4. HUMILITY AND OBEDIENCE:
   A cockerel and a hen—"The hen knows when it
   is dawn but she leaves the crowing to the cock."

5. MODERATION AND TEMPERANCE:
    Chicken catcher—"The result of continually
    chasing a chicken is that your hand touches
    some dirty ground."

6. PATRIOTISM:
    The Monitor Lizard—The monitor lizard says:
    "Mine is to help and build up, and not let
    down my state."

7. WARNING AGAINST INGRATITUDE:
    A cock near its water basin looking into the
    sky—"The cock in drinking water raises its head
    to God in thankfulness."

About the Author

KOFI ASARE OPOKU is a research fellow and teacher
of religion and ethics at the University of Ghana.
He attended the University of Ghana, Yale University
Divinity School, and the University of Bonn, Germany,
and has traveled extensively in the United States,
Europe, and West Africa. Mr. Opoku and his family
live in Legon, Ghana.

About the Illustrator

DINDGA McCANNON has won praise as the
author-illustrator of *Peaches* and as the illustrator of
three other Lothrop books: *Omar at Christmas,*
Sati the Rastifarian, and *Children of Night,* all written
by Edgar White.
   Ms. McCannon was born in Harlem, New York City.
She studied at the Art Students' League and at the
City University of New York and had her first
one-woman show when she was seventeen.